DATE		

WITHDRAWN

SCIENCE IN
ANCIENT EGYPT

VIEWPOINT SCHOOL

Given to the Library by

Mr. and Mrs. Irwin Plitt
in celebration of
Alexander's
January birthday
with love and pride.
February 1996

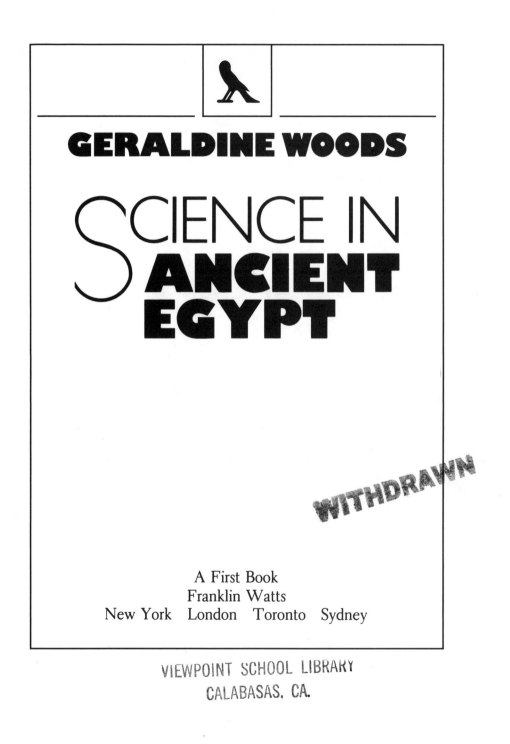

GERALDINE WOODS

SCIENCE IN ANCIENT EGYPT

A First Book
Franklin Watts
New York   London   Toronto   Sydney

Library of Congress Cataloging-in-Publication Data

Woods, Geraldine.
Science in Ancient Egypt / Geraldine Woods.
p.   cm. — (A First book)
Bibliography: p.
Includes index.
Summary: Discusses the achievements of the ancient Egyptians in
science, mathematics, astronomy, medicine, agriculture, and
technology.
ISBN 0-531-10486-9
1. Science—Egypt—History—Juvenile literature.   2. Engineering—
Egypt—History—Juvenile literature.   3. Science, Ancient—Juvenile
literature. [1. Science—Egypt—History. 2. Technology—Egypt—
History.   3. Science, Ancient.] I. Title.
Q127.E3W66   1988
509.32—dc19   87-23746   CIP   AC

For Tommy

CONTENTS

SCIENCE IN ANCIENT EGYPT

1

GEOGRAPHY AND ANCIENT EGYPTIAN SCIENCE

"Hail to thee, O Nile, that issues from the earth and comes to keep Egypt alive. . . ."

This prayer was written almost four thousand years ago by an unknown Egyptian. When it was composed, civilization in Egypt was already old. Human beings first began to live along the banks of the Nile about ten thousand years ago. They created a society that lasted longer than any other in history—twenty-seven centuries! Egyptian culture, science, and technology were shaped by the great river. In fact, an ancient Greek historian once called Egypt "the gift of the Nile."

The Nile winds through over 4,000 miles (6,400 km) of Africa before emptying into the Mediterranean Sea. Along most of its northern length it is surrounded by desert. It would be nearly impossible to create a great civilization in that forbidding land of sand and heat—impossible, that is, without the Nile.

The Nile River

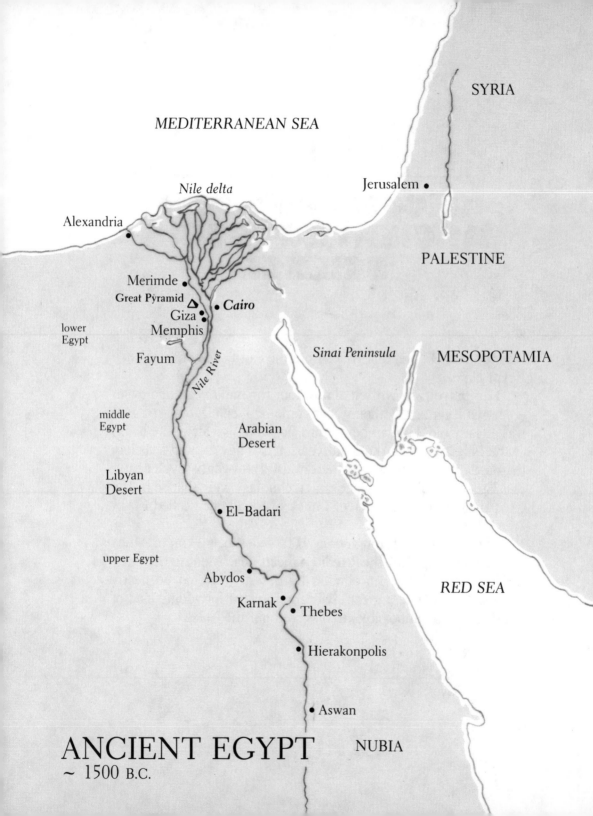

SYRIA

MEDITERRANEAN SEA

Nile delta

Jerusalem •

Alexandria •

PALESTINE

Merimde •

Great Pyramid △
Giza •   • *Cairo*
Memphis

lower
Egypt

MESOPOTAMIA

Fayum

Sinai Peninsula

Nile River

middle
Egypt

Arabian
Desert

Libyan
Desert

• El–Badari

upper Egypt

RED SEA

Abydos •

Karnak •
• Thebes

• Hierakonpolis

• Aswan

ANCIENT EGYPT
~ 1500 B.C.

NUBIA

The Nile is a strange river. For most of the year it flows peacefully to the sea. Every June, however, the river rises, fueled by spring rains that fall deep within Africa. Before modern dams were built, the Nile overflowed its banks onto the fields surrounding it. This watered the crops and also deposited extremely fertile silt that the river had been carrying in its currents. With good soil and enough water, Egyptian farming flourished.

So did Egyptian science. To take advantage of the Nile's water, the Egyptians invented irrigation. To time the flood, they made a calendar. To measure the flood, they created mathematical formulas. To sail on the Nile, they designed a variety of boats. To avoid its rapids, they learned how to dig canals.

The desert also contributed to the development of Egyptian culture. Other ancient societies were faced with the constant threat of invasion. The Mesopotamians, for example, lived on an open plain. They had to constantly guard against enemies from surrounding areas. A large part of the Mesopotamians' energy was devoted to warfare.

This was not true in Egypt. The desert was an excellent barrier between Egypt and foreign armies. From time to time, of course, war broke out, but in general the ancient Egyptians led a peaceful existence. This gave them time to develop art, design, crafts, science, and technology.

The Greek writer Philon wrote a book called *The Seven Wonders of the World*, a travel guide for ancient tourists. Although many of Egypt's achievements could be considered "wonders," only one made Philon's list. So we will begin our look at the science of ancient Egypt with its official wonder—the Great Pyramid.

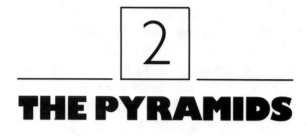

THE PYRAMIDS

A few years ago a popular book came out which claimed that the Egyptian pyramids were really built by visitors from outer space. The author had one main argument for this theory. In his view, the pyramids were so monumental that no ancient people could have built them without help from aliens. Scientists immediately proved that the pyramids could indeed be constructed by human beings, even those who lived forty-six hundred years ago. However, they did agree that these structures were a remarkable accomplishment.

Archeologists have identified the remains of over eighty pyramids in Egypt; all were tombs for **pharaohs** and other noble Egyptians. The step pyramid built for King Djoser about 2680 B.C. is the oldest. It is also the first large building ever constructed entirely of stone. According to an ancient Egyptian writing, the step design was meant to be "a staircase to heaven . . . for [the pharaoh] so that he may mount up to heaven thereby." As Egyptian builders became more skilled, they changed the steps into a true pyramid, the sacred sign for their sun god, Ra.

The Great Pyramid of the pharaoh Khufu (usually known by his Greek name, Cheops) is the largest. It covers 13 acres (5.2 ha)

The Great Pyramid

and contains 2,250,000 blocks of stone, averaging 5,000 pounds (over 2,000 kg). The Emperor Napoleon once calculated that the stone from Cheops's pyramid could build a wall 10 feet (3 m) high and 1 foot (30 cm) thick around the entire nation of France.

It's hard to imagine how anyone could construct such an enormous building, even in modern times. Moreover, only six simple machines were in existence at the time the pyramids were built—the lever, the inclined plane, the wedge, the wheel, the pulley, and the screw. The Egyptians employed only the first three in building the pyramids, although they may have been aware of the existence of the wheel and used it for other purposes.

PREPARING TO BUILD

The first step in building a pyramid was to clear the area of sand and gravel until the rock floor of the desert was exposed. The next task was to make the site perfectly level. Any structure consisting of so many tons of rock needs a solid base. Even a slight difference in height between one side of the pyramid and another could cause the entire structure to come crashing down.

How do you make sure that 13 acres of land are perfectly flat, without modern surveyors' instruments like compasses and sextants? The Egyptians used water. They knew that free-flowing water always forms a level surface. So the Egyptians dug a network of trenches that crisscrossed the base area of the pyramid. They flooded the trenches, then marked the water line on the sides. After draining the trenches, laborers cut the surface of the ground down to the watermarks. Lastly, they filled in the trenches with rubble.

Meanwhile, the architects were drawing the plan of the building on clay tablets. Although a pyramid appears to be a solid mass of stone, it actually contains a number of tunnels and rooms. There was a chamber for the pharaoh's sarcophagus (a stone coffin) and

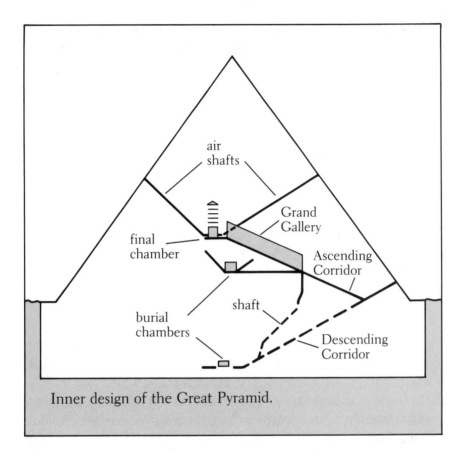

air shafts

Grand Gallery

final chamber

Ascending Corridor

shaft

burial chambers

Descending Corridor

Inner design of the Great Pyramid.

another for the treasures that the ruler would need in the next life. A passage from the outside was built so that the pharaoh's body could be brought to its resting place. In some pyramids, chambers for the pharaoh's wife and her treasures were also included.

Many pyramids also contained false tunnels and empty rooms. All these interior chambers made things harder for the tomb robbers. Unfortunately they also created difficulties for the builders. The pyramids were built in layers. Once the thousands of blocks that made up each level of the pyramid were in place, it was almost impossible to move them. Therefore the builders had to be extremely careful to plan the proper position of tunnel and tomb openings in each layer of rock.

The architects were also in charge of ordering their building materials. The pyramids were constructed around a core of limestone, which could be quarried in the western desert only a short distance from the building site. The interior chambers were usually made of granite, a harder stone. Granite was quarried at Aswan, about 500 miles (800 km) up river from the tombs. The outer surfaces of the pyramids were covered with pure white limestone, which came from across the Nile near Cairo in eastern Egypt. The planners listed the number, type, and measurements of the stones they needed for the project. The scribes sent copies to the quarries, where work gangs were waiting to fill the orders.

CUTTING STONE

Ancient Egyptian quarries were not equipped with the dynamite, power drills, and forklift trucks that make modern stoneworkers' tasks easier. Ancient Egyptian stoneworkers had only a few primitive tools available to cut into solid rock—mainly chisels, saws, mallets, hammers, and wedges. The chisels and saws were metal; mallets and wedges were shaped from wood; and hammers were made from rock laced to a wooden handle. With these tools Egyptian workers cut millions of blocks of stone.

Before cutting, workers first drew marks on the rock to outline each block. Then with chisels and mallets they chipped a series of small cracks into the stone. Next, the workers hammered wedges into the cracks and soaked the area with water. As the water was absorbed by the dry wood, the wedge swelled and split the rock. Some experts believe that the Egyptians also heated the cracks and then cooled them suddenly with water. The fast change in temperature caused the rock to split.

This unfinished obelisk in the quarries at Aswan
is 120 feet (37 m) long and would have weighed
over 1,200 tons (540 kg) on completion. Work
on the obelisk was abandoned around 1500 B.C.
because of a crack that developed.

Ton after ton of rock was removed from the desert cliffs, and huge caves were formed. The supervisors instructed their workers to leave pillars of stone uncut in order to support the cave roofs. As the caves deepened, the strong Egyptian sun could not penetrate. The supervisors then provided oil lamps—shallow dishes filled with oil and lit by a wick lying on the side of the dish.

TRANSPORTING AND
FINISHING THE BLOCKS

The rough-cut blocks of stone had to be transported to the building site, where they would be finished and set in place. It was not easy to move boulders weighing two and a half tons each, especially without wheels. To raise each block, the workers probably tied ropes of palm fiber to it and then tilted one side with a lever. Or, the Egyptians may have used a weight arm to lift the blocks. A weight arm is made of heavy timber. It has a central post and two arms, one short and one long. A sling is slipped under the block and attached to the short arm. Small rocks are placed on a platform attached to the long arm until they almost balance the weight of the block. The block rises when the long arm is tipped.

Once the block was raised, a wooden sled was quickly slipped underneath. A team of men pulled the sled out of the cave, following a path of logs which were laid to keep the sled from sinking into the sand. The blocks were brought to the Nile and loaded on barges, which carried them to the dock.

When they arrived, the blocks still had to be smoothed and cut to exact size before being placed in the pyramid. Workers cut away the larger bumps with saws or chisels and mallets. Then they rubbed the surface with rough stone or a lump of extremely hard rock called dolerite.

Every part of the block was tested with a **boning rod** to see if the surface was level. A boning rod was made of three pegs of equal height. A cord was attached to the top of two of the pegs. Two workers rested these pegs on the stone and stretched the cord tightly. Another worker moved the third peg back and forth across the block. If the surface was even, the third peg fit perfectly between the stone and the cord. When bulges were detected, workers smoothed the stone. The corners of each block were also measured to be sure that they were perfectly square. The workers used wooden right angles and knocked away any extra rock with chisels or pieces of flint. It must have taken days of backbreaking labor to make sure every block was exactly the right shape.

CONSTRUCTING THE PYRAMID

Many pyramids contained underground rooms. Before construction could begin, these chambers had to be excavated. To make the digging easier, the Egyptians probably worked with caissons. Caissons, which are still used in the construction of tunnels today, are hollow cylinders made of stone and brick. The caisson is placed on the site, and the diggers work inside it. As the dirt is removed the caisson is pushed forward. Its strong walls keep the hole from caving in. Laborers following the caisson reinforce the walls of the excavation with stone.

After the Egyptians dug the underground chambers, it was time to actually move the pyramid stones into position. It was the enormity of this task that made some people imagine alien building crews working from spaceships. After all, it could not have been easy to place such giant chunks of rock into even one layer—and the pyramids were built many stories high. The blocks were dragged into place on sleds or rollers made of logs. To carry blocks to the higher layers, huge ramps made of mud and sand were built on the sides of the pyramids. Workers probably sprinkled water or oil over the stones to make them slide more easily over one another. The blocks fitted together so well that no mortar was needed to

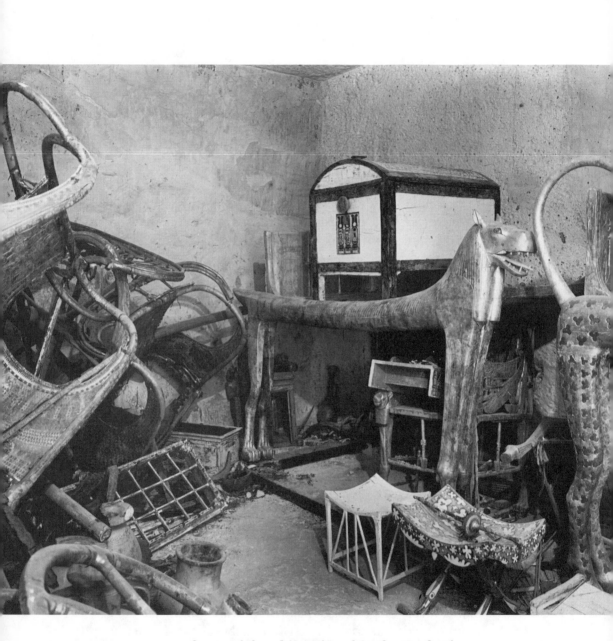

*Some of the objects found in the tomb of
Tutankhamun, better known as King Tut*

hold them in place. In most places, the seam between blocks is so tight that not even the blade of a knife could be inserted. Some joints are only 0.0001 inch (0.0003 cm) wide!

As each layer was finished, a surveyor checked that the edges were perfectly square. A plumb line was also used to see that each layer was rising at the correct angle. A plumb line is simply a cord and a pointed stone. The cord, with the stone attached to the end, is hung until it just grazes the earth. When the cord stops swinging it always makes a right angle with the ground.

When it was time to put a roof over an inner chamber, workers filled the room with dirt. They set the roof stones in place and then removed the dirt through the chamber's doorway. When the room was empty, stoneworkers finished the interior of the room, usually with granite. The same method was used to create the roofs of the pyramid's tunnels.

The very top of the pyramid was the capstone, a perfectly pointed stone with a plug on its lower side. The plug fit into a hole on the preceding layer. Once the capstone was in place, stoneworkers began to smooth and polish the outside of the pyramid. As they traveled toward the base, other workers removed the dirt ramps. When the last ramp was removed, the pyramid was finished—a path to heaven for the pharaoh, and a monument to the earthly labor of the Egyptians.

3

MATHEMATICS

Over thirty-five hundred years ago, Ahmes the Moonborn wrote a book called *How to Obtain Information About All Things Mysterious and Dark.* The "mysterious and dark" subject matter was mathematics. Ahmes's volume contained forty sample problems illustrating the multiplication and division of fractions. He also explained how to calculate the area of a circle, square, and triangle and how to determine the volume of some solids.

This arithmetic would be simple for most of today's fifth-graders. Yet to Ahmes it was a great secret. That's because in ancient Egypt general math was not taught to all schoolchildren. Many people knew a few facts related to their jobs. Surveyors could measure a right angle, and traders could add the weights and values of their goods. However, mathematical theory was usually studied only by those who held high positions in Egyptian society—usually priests and government officials. Their knowledge came from practical needs; the government collected taxes and organized landownership, and the priests calculated the actions of the Nile god Hapi.

As early as 3000 B.C., the Egyptians were able to predict the size of the Nile's flood. They constructed nilometers, which were

Scribes recording the harvest

stone gauges with lines to measure the amount the river rose. The nilometers were placed near the Elephantine Island. The priests knew that a water depth of more than 28 feet (8.5 m) at the city of Memphis meant huge floods and disaster for the country. Less than 21 feet (6.4 m), on the other hand, foretold too little water and a poor harvest. About 25 feet (7.6 m) was the best; the Nile would bring just enough water for the crops.

COUNTING

None of this could be determined without a system of counting and measuring. The earliest math in Egypt probably began over five thousand years ago when people chipped notches on wood or stone to record the passing of time. Later, symbols were created to

stand for different numbers. Like most number systems, the Egyptian method of counting gave special importance to the number 10 and to multiples of 10. This is probably because human beings have ten fingers to count with!

The Egyptians did not always follow logical order in writing numbers. The symbols for 1,492 could be mixed in any pattern, as long as they added up to the correct total. This was because the Egyptians did not base their arithmetic on place value, as we do. In our system, 321 is very different from 123. The symbols 0 through 9 are always the same, but the place determines whether we mean 3 hundreds or 3 units.

The Egyptians simply used different symbols for hundreds and units. They also had no real symbol for zero in math, although a blank space was occasionally used to represent the lack of a number. This made their arithmetic more complicated and difficult to do. To add 765 and 321, for example, the Egyptians had to deal with these two large numbers without breaking them down into smaller, easier problems. In our system the addition is done by columns: we add 5 and 1, 6 and 2, and 7 and 3 to arrive at 1,086.

The Egyptians did have fractions, although they only understood fractions that were "one part of" the whole (1/10, 1/8, 1/5, and so forth). If any other fraction was needed, the Egyptians calculated with a set of numbers. Three-sevenths might be written as $1/7 + 1/7 + 1/7$ or as $1/4 + 1/7 + 1/28$.

A nilometer with
markings to mea-
sure the height
of the river

27

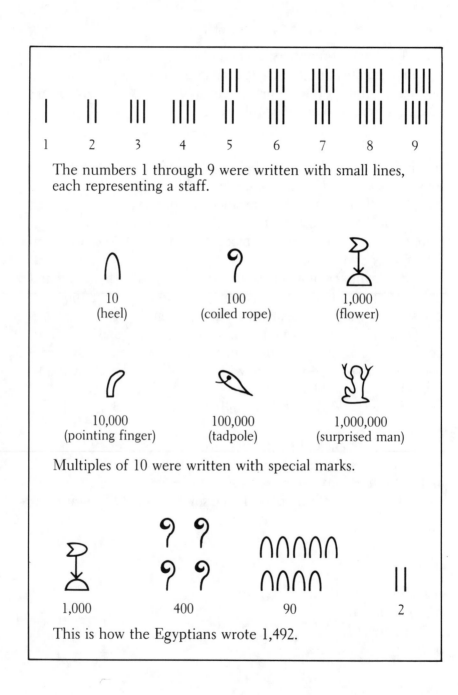

The numbers 1 through 9 were written with small lines, each representing a staff.

10
(heel)

100
(coiled rope)

1,000
(flower)

10,000
(pointing finger)

100,000
(tadpole)

1,000,000
(surprised man)

Multiples of 10 were written with special marks.

1,000

400

90

2

This is how the Egyptians wrote 1,492.

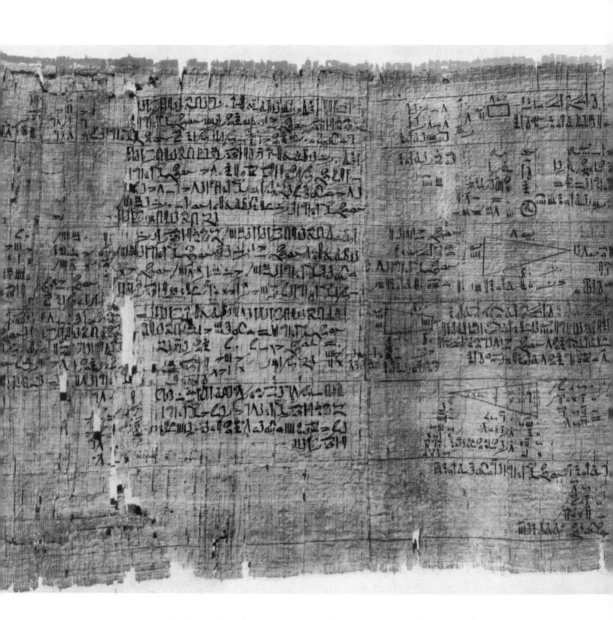

A section of the Rhind Papyrus, an important mathematical document dating from almost four thousand years ago

There was a special sign that meant "one part of." Here are three Egyptian fractions:

is "one part of ten," or 1/10

is "one part of seven," or 1/7

is "one part of nine," or 1/9

When measuring grain, other signs were used. These were based on the drawing of the eye of the god Horus. With this shortcut, a surveyor would simply draw Horus's eyebrow for the fraction ⅛ or the eyeball for ¼.

MEASURING

The earliest measurements were based on the human body. Since the pharaoh, Egypt's ruler, was the most important person in the country, the first measurements came from him. A **cubit** was the length of his forearm from the elbow to the tip of his middle finger. The width of his palm and the width of four fingers together were also used.

The problem, of course, was that all human bodies are different. Very soon the Egyptians realized that they needed a standard. Official measuring sticks were created, although the old body-part names were kept. A cubit was defined as 7 palms; 4 digits (fingers) equaled 1 palm. There were also two types of cubits—the royal,

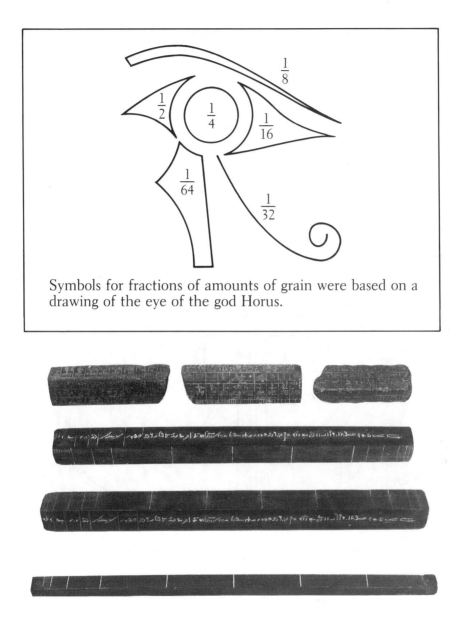

Symbols for fractions of amounts of grain were based on a drawing of the eye of the god Horus.

$\frac{1}{8}$

$\frac{1}{2}$ $\frac{1}{4}$ $\frac{1}{16}$

$\frac{1}{64}$ $\frac{1}{32}$

Cubits

which was about 21 inches (53 cm), and the everyday, which was a little shorter. Measuring sticks marked with cubits, palms, digits, and fractions have been found in Egyptian tombs.

Weight measures have also been found. The Egyptians originally created a system based on the weight of a single grain of wheat. Later, standard stone weights that could be used on a balance scale were made.

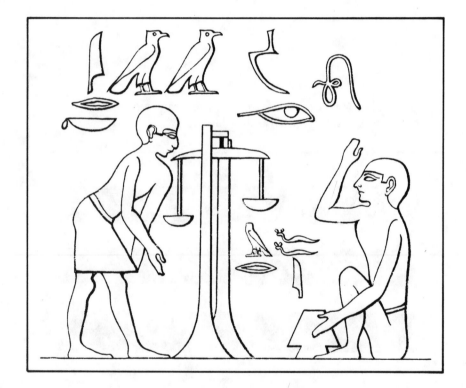

The earliest-known depiction of
the use of a balance. This picture, carved
in stone, dates from about 2500 B.C.

ARITHMETIC

The Egyptians knew how to add and subtract. They could also multiply and divide, but their methods were very different from ours. To multiply 23 by 13, for example, the Egyptians made two columns of numbers. The first column always began with 1, and the second began with the number to be multiplied (in this case 23). Each line of the columns doubled the line before:

$$
\begin{array}{ll}
1 & 23 \\
2 & 46 \\
4 & 92 \\
8 & 184
\end{array}
$$

Then they added the numbers in the first column that equaled the multiplier:

$$1 + 4 + 8 = 13$$

Lastly, they added each number's partner:

$$23 + 92 + 184 = 299$$

In other words, they added 1×23, 4×23, and 8×23. The answer is 13×23, or 299.

Division was also done with columns. To divide 48 by 8, for example, the columns began with 1 and 8 and doubled on each line:

$$
\begin{array}{ll}
1 & 8 \\
2 & 16 \\
4 & 32 \\
8 & 64
\end{array}
$$

Measuring land using a knotted rope

Then, by trial and error, the Egyptians would add the numbers in the second column to find which numbers totaled 48. In this case, 16 + 32 = 48. The answer is the sum of their partners, 2 + 4, or 6. In effect, the Egyptians broke the division problem into parts. They found out the answer to 16 divided by 8 (which is 2) and 32 divided by 8 (which is 4). If the number could not be equaled exactly, the closest numbers were used and the remainders were expressed as fractions.

AREAS AND ANGLES

Since the Nile wiped out the boundaries of each farmer's fields once every year, the Egyptians had to become expert surveyors in order to redraw property lines. Surveyors, who were called "rope stretchers," probably worked with a set of knotted ropes. Ropes laid out in a straight line were used for simple measures. Distances across a stream or other obstacles could also be calculated. Early on, an unknown Egyptian figured out that a triangle measuring 3,

4, 5 or 5, 12, 13 on its sides would always contain a right angle. By sighting with a right angle and constructing an imaginary triangle, distances could be determined indirectly.

The Egyptians measured their property carefully partly to keep peace between neighbors and partly to calculate how much grain each farmer was required to pay as taxes. Since the amount was based on the area of each field, the Egyptians became skilled at computing the area of squares, rectangles, triangles, and circles. This was fine for fields that fit these shapes exactly. However, most fields did not. Eventually the Egyptians discovered that the best way to measure an irregular piece of land was to divide it into triangles. A field shaped like the one shown below could be calculated as the sum of triangles A, B, C, and D.

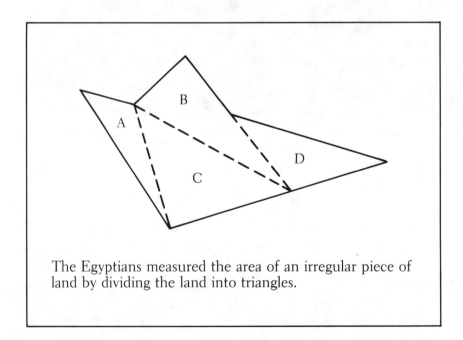

The Egyptians measured the area of an irregular piece of land by dividing the land into triangles.

MATH AND
THE PYRAMIDS

In constructing colossal pyramids for their kings, the Egyptians used many techniques based on mathematical ideas. Some of these were passed down in a sort of early engineering textbook—a scroll which explained the building problems connected with large stone buildings and monuments.

Most Egyptian "building math" involved little more than some rope and a few pegs. In fact, the ceremony marking the beginning of a new pyramid was actually called Put-ser—"to stretch a cord." During Put-ser the pharaoh held a golden mallet and a rope while reciting, "I hold the handle of the mallet; I grasp the cord with Seshata [goddess of the stars] . . . I establish the four corners of the temple."

There are several ways the Egyptians may have used the mallet and rope to make the corners of their buildings absolutely square. The most likely way involved a rope stretched between two pegs. The builders may have tied equal pieces of cord to the two pegs and then swung the cords in an arc. The arcs cross each

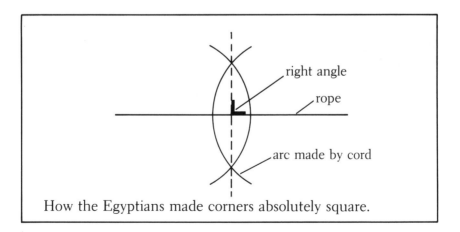

How the Egyptians made corners absolutely square.

other at two points. A line drawn between these two points crosses the rope at right angles. It also divides the rope into two equal parts. This is illustrated on the previous page.

Although the Egyptians were good mathematicians, they never created a theory of algebra. Algebra is a branch of mathematics in which problems are often written in the form of equations. The equations contain letters which represent unknown quantities. A typical equation might be $2x + 3y = 12$. The aim is to calculate the value of the unknowns, x and y. By trial and error, the Egyptians did figure out how to solve problems with unknown quantities. However, they never developed a series of rules for this process. Nevertheless, their practical math was the most advanced of its age.

ASTRONOMY
AND
TIMEKEEPING

Every ancient Egyptian child knew that the sun god Ra sailed one boat across the sky every day and another through the waters under the earth during the dark hours. The children knew that the stars were also boats which blew through the heavens the same way sailboats blew up and down the Nile. They were aware that the five days of festivals everyone enjoyed each year were a gift from the god Thoth. Thoth had played a dice game with the moon and won some of its light, which he fashioned into five extra days.

Now that we are in the space age, these myths may seem silly. Yet the stories contain a surprising amount of scientific knowledge. The tales of Ra's boat and the stars show that the Egyptians observed the movements of the sun and the constellations. Thoth's game was a fanciful way of explaining the change Egypt made between a calendar based on the moon and one based on the sun.

SIRIUS AND THE CALENDAR

The ancient Egyptians' knowledge of astronomy and time started in a very natural way. Like all primitive people, the earliest Egyptians probably first kept time by marking the passage of days on a stick. Later, they probably reckoned time by the most obvious change in their lives—the annual flood of the Nile.

Very soon, however, they turned to the sky. Just about all ancient peoples were stargazers. Without strong artificial light, the nights are darker and the stars show up more clearly. And in a society that has little else for entertainment, the sky can put on the most spectacular show in town!

The brightest object in the night sky, of course, is the moon. The moon's cycles are very short. In only 29 or 30 days the moon grows, becomes full, shrinks, and disappears. Perhaps that is why most ancient people, including the early Egyptians, created a calendar of "moons," or months. Each time a new moon appeared, a new month began. Since this occurs every 29½ days, each month was 29 or 30 days long. Twelve months were counted as one year. Unfortunately, there are only 354 days in this type of year, and the extra days add up quickly. Within a few years, a winter month has turned into a summer month!

The Egyptians solved this problem by switching to a solar, or sun, calendar, which grew out of their observations of the stars. At some point in Egypt's dim past, people began to notice that the stars moved across the sky according to regular patterns. (Of course, it is really the earth that moves, not the stars, but that fact was not discovered until thousands of year later.) The Egyptians, a methodical people, began to keep charts of the stars' movements.

They named constellations after animals they were familiar with, like crocodiles, oxen, and hippos. They also divided the heavenly bodies into three categories. "The Unwearied" were actually planets; they got this name because they never stopped moving. Although they had no telescopes, the Egyptians observed Jupiter, Saturn, Venus, Mars, and perhaps Mercury. "The Imperishables" were circumpolar stars, those which appeared to revolve around the North Pole and did not set. The Egyptians believed

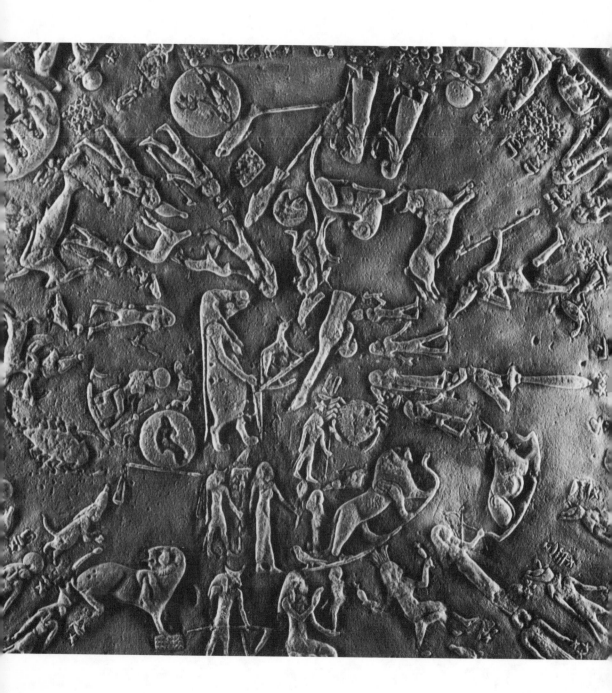

that the Imperishables were located in the Heavenly Fields, where their kings lived an eternal life. The last type, "the Indestructibles," consisted of thirty-six specially chosen stars which eventually gave their names to the Egyptian weeks.

Around 3000 B.C., Sirius, the Dog Star, attracted attention because it was brighter than all the other stars. Yet sometimes Sirius vanished. Then it would appear again, just for a few minutes, at dawn. Each day thereafter Sirius would stay in the sky for a longer period of time, until it disappeared again. Soon someone observed that Sirius always returned just before the Nile was ready to overflow its banks.

This knowledge was extremely valuable. All the other methods the Egyptians had tried were fine for recording time. However, Sirius's movements gave them the ability to predict an event. Knowing that the Nile was about to overflow allowed the Egyptians to move their houses and livestock to higher ground and to prepare for the planting season. So the Egyptians based their calendar on Sirius, and calculated a year as the time between one reappearance of the star and another.

This was a lucky choice. Sirius's cycle is 365¼ days long— exactly the same amount of time it takes the earth to revolve once around the sun. So the Egyptian calendar followed the seasons correctly, and avoided the traveling months of the moon-based calendar.

The Egyptians subdivided their calendar into three seasons: the flooding of the Nile, the planting season, and the dry season. They also created decans, ten-day weeks which were named for the Indestructible star that was prominent in the sky during that period.

Zodiac ceiling in a temple

The astronomers also decided that three weeks would equal one month—and that created a problem. Twelve months of thirty days each total 360. Five days short! That's where the legend of Thoth comes in. The five extra days that Thoth won from the moon were given as holidays not belonging to any particular month. The year now equaled 365 days. This was still one-fourth of a day short, but it was the best calendar in the ancient world and a major improvement on the moon-based calendar.

ASTRONOMY
AND ARCHITECTURE

The Egyptians also used their knowledge of astronomy to solve engineering problems. Architects planning a pyramid always made sure that the four sides of the building faced exactly north, south, east, and west. They may have done this by building a tall circle of stone on the site of the pyramid. Inside the circle a priest marked the spots where a star rose in the evening and set in the morning. The point halfway between these two marks is true north.

The ancient builders also positioned other structures according to the heavens. The Temple of Amun at Karnak, for example, has a long line of columns. An observer looking along this line at dawn on midsummer day will see the rising sun directly between the last two columns. The pyramid of Cheops contains an air shaft leading to the north face. The north star of ancient times could be sighted through this tunnel.

The Egyptians also knew how to determine directions by the sun. The sun rises in the southeast in winter and in the northeast in

The Temple of
Amun at Karnak

44

summer. The Egyptians marked the direction of the rising sun on midwinter and midwinter day—the halfway point of each season. By halving the angle formed by these two lines they found due east. A simpler, but less exact method, was to build a tall column. The shadow of the column at noon points north; east and west can be found by crossing the shadow with a right-angle line.

CLOCKS AND TIMEKEEPING

The sun's shadow was also a convenient method for marking the passage of hours. The Egyptians' shadow clock was like a sundial, but its design was slightly different. A shadow clock had one flat arm and one upright arm. The crossbar was positioned pointing due east at dawn. The upright arm cast a shadow on the flat arm; the longest shadow marked the sixth hour before noon. At midday, the shadow was shortest. At that time the clock had to be turned around; during the afternoon the shadows lengthened on the bar.

The Egyptians also used water clocks. The simplest was just a large bowl with a hole in the bottom. As the water flowed out, hour lines on the side of the bowl appeared. The lines had to be calculated carefully to allow for the sloping sides of the bowl. There is more water in one inch at the wide rim of the bowl than there is at the narrow bottom. The lines also had to take into account the difference in flow rate as the bowl empties. A bowl filled to the top will leak more quickly than one that is almost empty. The Egyptians were unable to calculate the change in flow rate perfectly; therefore their water clocks were not entirely correct.

The Egyptians named their hours instead of numbering them. Lunch was eaten at "the time of the perfume of the mouth." However, Egyptian hours were not like ours. Every hour in our day is

A shadow clock from the tenth century B.C.

exactly 60 minutes long, no matter when it occurs. Egyptian hours changed according to the time of the year. This is because the Egyptians divided both day and night into twelve equal parts. Since the length of a day changes with the seasons, so does the length of one-twelfth of a day. In winter the sun rises later and sets earlier than it does during the summer. Therefore the twelve Egyptian winter-day hours were shorter than the twelve summer-day hours. The opposite is true of the night hours.

These changing hours were called temporal, or temporary hours. Egyptian clocks had to be constructed around these temporal hours. The water clock, for example, had markings for both summer and winter. The winter night was 14 fingers of water long, while the summer night lasted for only 12 fingers.

The design of Egyptian clocks was based on accurate observation and an ingenious use of common materials. These same qualities may be found throughout Egyptian science. As a matter of fact, they are also typical of the ancients' approach to almost every aspect of their daily life.

MEDICINE

Egyptian workers trying to mummify a corpse always faced one difficulty. The mummy was supposed to provide a place for a wandering spirit to return to its body. Therefore, the body had to be kept in perfect condition—eternally. If the body decayed, the soul would be homeless. However, the Egyptians knew of no way to preserve the body without performing an operation. Yet it was considered disgraceful to scar a corpse. The solution? A special priest was brought in just to make the cut. The others waited, holding small stones. As soon as the body was open, they threw the stones at the priest and drove him out of the room.

Although the Egyptians made a ceremony of scorning the men who did these operations, the world owes these priests a great deal of thanks. For it was these men who allowed the Egyptians to study anatomy, the structure of a human body. This detailed knowledge, which no other people of that time had, made the Egyptians the best physicians in the ancient world. The Persian emperors Cyrus and Darius, as well as rulers in many other countries, relied on Egyptian physicians. Homer, an ancient Greek poet, praised Egyptian doctors in his epic *The Odyssey*. The Greeks identified their god of medicine, Asklepios, with a real

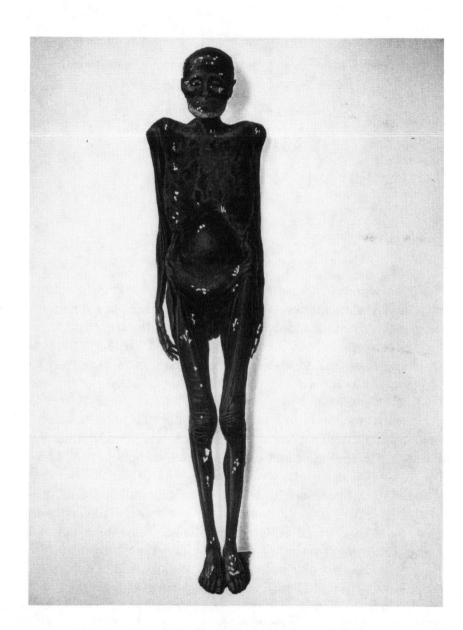

A mummy unrolled April 6, 1833

Egyptian. He was the nobleman Imhotep, who lived about 2600 B.C. Imhotep was not only a good physician but also the architect who designed the first pyramid.

Another Greek, the historian Herodotus, believed that the Egyptians were one of the healthiest nations in the ancient world. He explained that, "Each physician applies himself to one disease only, and not more." Herodotus exaggerated; there were doctors who treated anyone who was ill. However, just as in modern times, the Egyptians also had many specialists. One scroll refers to the "Palace Eye Physician" and the "Palace Stomach-Bowel Physician."

MAKING A MUMMY

The custom of making mummies probably began because of Egypt's extremely dry climate. Early Egyptians buried their dead in shallow graves; some bodies were probably uncovered after severe sandstorms. The dead bodies that reappeared probably looked almost as good as new because the dry, hot weather would have prevented their decay. Eventually this natural process became an important part of the Egyptian religion. The Egyptians believed that a preserved body could go on to another world with the spirit of the dead person. This religious idea may have inspired the Egyptians to look for techniques to guarantee preservation.

The mummification process the Egyptians developed was designed to remove water from the body, since dry material is less likely to decay. The dead body was opened by a priest and the heart, liver, and other organs were removed. The body cavity and the separate parts were washed with wine; the alcohol in the wine is a natural germ-killer. Then the body was packed with **natron**, a salt compound. The organs were placed in jars containing more natron. After about two months, the salt had drawn most of the remaining moisture from the body and the body parts. The body

and its organs were then treated with resin (a sealant) and wax. The organs were placed in jars again for burial, and the body was wrapped in linen bandages.

Surprisingly, modern scientists believe that this complicated process was not that effective. The corpses were preserved, but this was mainly due to the dry Egyptian air—not to the natron and bandages!

THE FIRST MEDICAL BOOKS

Not all ancient Egyptian knowledge of medicine came from the study of mummies. The Egyptians were also careful observers of the living; they noted symptoms and experimented with a large number of drugs and treatments. Successful methods were taught to new generations of doctors, often by means of scrolls. These scrolls were the first medical textbooks in history.

One scroll lists heart conditions and another discusses diseases of women and children. A "first aid" scroll explains how to treat injuries, and the "recipe scrolls" give directions for making medicines. To modern readers, some texts seem to wander off the subject. A few volumes tackled insect repellents, housekeeping, and even beauty tips. Included in one book dated 1550 B.C. is a recipe for a wrinkle remover made of ox gall and powdered ostrich egg.

Another scroll is *The Book of Surgery*. It dates from about 1550 B.C., but it is actually a copy of a document which was composed about 2250 B.C. Forty-eight cases are listed in order by body part from the head down. Each has a title, instructions for examination

Drawings of mummified animals found in Egyptian tombs

53

of the patient, diagnosis, and treatment. In order to help ancient readers understand the even-more-ancient book, the writer gives an explanation of terms that might be unfamiliar. "Moor the patient at his mooring stakes," for example, is defined as keeping the person immobile. Cases are divided into those that are treatable and those that are "not to be treated" because they are hopeless. Case number 10 discusses a wound above the eyebrow:

> Examination
> If you examine a man having a wound in the top of his eyebrow, penetrating to the bone, you should [feel] the wound and draw [it] together for him . . . with stitching.
>
> Diagnosis
> You should say . . . "One having a wound in his eyebrow. An ailment which I will treat."
>
> Treatment
> Now after you have stitched it, you should bind fresh meat upon it the first day. If you find that the stitching of his wound is loose, you should draw it together for him with two strips of plaster, and you should treat it with grease and honey every day until he recovers.

From *The Book of Surgery* and other scrolls we have learned much about the abilities of Egyptian physicians. It seems that their reputation was justified. The Egyptians knew how to set broken bones and attach a splint. They sawed through the skull with copper tools to treat head wounds, and they were among the first to use bandages and compresses. They expected cuts to become infected (they had no antibiotics), but they knew how to tie the edges of a wound together to reduce scarring. One papyrus even refers to skin grafts (transferring skin from one part of the body to another), but no details are given on how it was done.

EARLY DRUGGISTS

Parents who give castor oil to their children as a cure for upset stomachs are following an ancient tradition. Thousands of years ago the Egyptians chewed castor berries for the same ailment. Castor berries were just one of the remedies in the ancient Egyptian "medicine cabinet." Drugs were also made from many other plants and spices such as acacia, anise, cassia, cumin, poppy flowers, and saffron. The Egyptians also made compounds of copper, feldspar, sulfur, sodium bicarbonate and other minerals. Animal products were common; parts or all of various birds, pigs, crocodiles, and even ants were prescribed. To make these mixtures easier to swallow, the Egyptians mixed them with milk, honey, wine, or beer. Creams and ointments were based on goose grease, honey, or animal fat.

How effective were these remedies? They varied. Patients with night blindness were probably helped by eating the liver their doctor prescribed; until recently cod liver oil, which is rich in vitamins, was given for the same problem. However, the treatment for nearsightedness (honey, lead, and water from a pig's eye injected into the patient's ear) did no good at all. Nor did the salve of turtle brains prescribed as a cure for cross-eyes and the "toes of a dog, date pits, and hoof of a donkey" given for baldness.

Still, the Egyptians did discover a remarkable number of drugs. Cranky babies were given pods of the poppy plant mixed with "fly dirt which is on the wall." Since poppies supply opium, a powerful sedative, the children undoubtedly calmed down. (The fly dirt had nothing to do with the cure!) Hartshorn, which is powdered deer antler, was mixed with birds' legs and other ingredients and used for many ailments. Today, doctors prescribe "spirits of hartshorn"—an ammonia mixture—for several conditions. Calcium phosphate, which can be obtained from hartshorn, is also an ingredient in many modern medicines. Earaches were treated with a mixture of salt and hot wine, which is similar to modern eardrops containing alcohol and boric powder. The Egyptians also used acacia and honey as a form of birth control. These two substances form lactic acid when mixed. Lactic acid is an ingredient in some of today's birth control products.

DENTISTRY

Hesi Re was one of the world's first dentists. According to his tomb inscription, which dates from about 2600 B.C., he was "Chief of Toothers and Physicians." He was probably a very busy man. Evidence suggests that almost everyone in ancient Egypt had to cope with toothaches at one time or another. Scientists studying

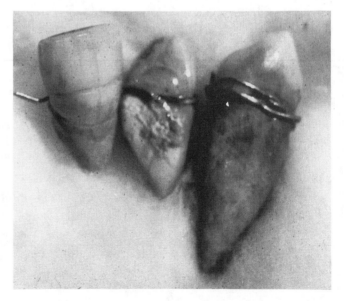

The first known set of "false" teeth

mummies and other remains have found that the teeth were often infected or worn down to the gum line. This may be because Egyptian grain was ground between stones and kept in open storage bins. The grain may have contained particles of sand and dirt that actually sandpapered the teeth while it was eaten.

Luckily, the Egyptians had some knowledge of dentistry. They knew how to fill cavities and treat infections. A jawbone dated 2800 B.C. shows a hole under a molar. The jaw was probably pierced to allow the pus from an infection to drain. Also, a forty-five-hundred-year-old skull has the earliest known set of false teeth. But in this case the "false" teeth used were real—three real teeth, held together by gold wire, appear to have been anchored to a hole drilled in another tooth. This was probably more effective than a glue for loose teeth described in one scroll—a paste of ochre (a red mineral), crushed seeds, and honey. The same book prescribes a mixture of beans, dates, and milk for sore gums, a remedy that also proved useless.

MANY SUCCESSES—
AND SOME FAILURES

Although remarkably advanced, Egyptian medicine had many gaps. Egyptian doctors understood the anatomy of a dead body, but they did not always realize how the living parts functioned. During the process of creating a mummy, for example, the brain was not saved; it was not considered as important as the other organs! Although they knew that the pulse and heartbeat were related, the Egyptians had only one word for muscles and blood vessels. They believed that both were responsible for movement. (One scroll says that "The beginning of the science of the physician [is] to know the movement of the heart; there are vessels attached to it for every movement of the body.") They also thought the hollow blood vessels carried many different substances: air, water, blood, semen, urine, and solid wastes.

The Egyptians also mixed science, religion, and magic when they practiced medicine. It was not unusual for physicians to be given the title of magician. A doctor would often recite spells over a clay statue and then place it above the patient's body. The physician might also draw magic circles around the house or hold a special seal above the patient's head.

Sometimes spells were prescribed. Certain words had to be recited every few hours—just like taking doses of medicine! Often these were prayers to the goddess Isis, who had once healed the god Osiris. Sometimes the prescription was a chant intended to encourage positive thinking. Someone with eye disease, for example, might say, "The crocodile is weak and powerless." According to Egyptian myth, the crocodile stole the eye of the sun and was therefore responsible for eye ailments. At other times the disease itself was addressed. A cure for the common cold was this spell:

> Flow out, poison nose, flow out, son of poison nose! You who breaks bones, destroys the skull, digs in the bone marrow and makes the seven holes in the head ill!

Of course, the Egyptians had no luck with that annoying disease. But that gives them something in common with us; modern medical science can't cure colds either!

WRITING
AND
AGRICULTURE

Some ancient Egyptian career advice:

> Behold, there is no calling wherein a man hath no master
> save that of the scribe, and he is himself the master.
> > —Instruction from Akhthoy to his son Piopi
> > on the first day of school, 1500 B.C.

> Make the most of all my land. . . . dig the ground with
> your nose in the work.
> > —Letter from Imhotep to his son Yahmose,
> > about 2000 B.C.

There is no record of whether Piopi and the farmer's son took their
fathers' advice. If they did, they participated in two of ancient
Egypt's greatest achievements: writing and agriculture.

WRITING

For over a thousand years, people looked at the writing on Egyptian monuments, scrolls, and tombs and wondered what it meant. Was it prayers, official records, magic spells, stories, shopping lists? In the end, it turned out to be all of these, although no one knew until a broken slab of black rock was found in the Egyptian delta in 1799. The slab, called the Rosetta Stone, contains words in both Egyptian and Greek. It was the first clue to the meaning of Egyptian picture writing, or **hieroglyphs**, since the ancient scribes had stopped using them so many centuries before.

It took the Frenchman Jean François Champollion over twenty years to figure out the secret of the Rosetta Stone. He uncovered a very complex system of writing. Although no one knows for sure exactly how Egyptian hieroglyphs developed, scholars believe they began as actual pictures. One simply drew whatever he or she wanted to say. At some point those pictures became stylized; many details were left out, and those that were included were drawn with as few strokes as possible. The pictures were also standardized. A man walking was always shown in the same way, and only one kind of mouth was drawn.

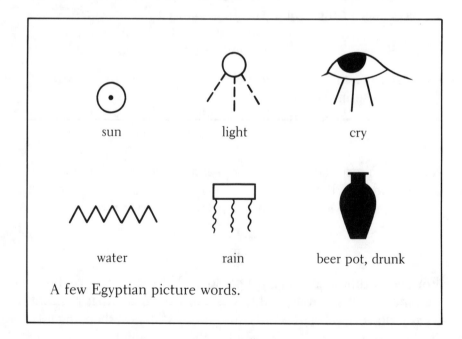

A few Egyptian picture words.

The Rosetta Stone. The lower section is Greek writing;
the top section is hieroglyphics;
the middle section is another type of Egyptian writing.

Some pictures had more than one meaning. This sign, for example, means "hill":

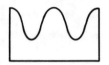

Since Egypt is a very flat country, the same sign is also used for the word *foreign*.

It was probably later that the signs came to stand for sounds as well as whole words. Scribes trying to express ideas that could not be drawn easily may have created little picture puzzles (like sketching a bee and a leaf for the word *belief*). Eventually, there were hieroglyphs for all the consonant sounds in the Egyptian language. Some pictures stood for one letter; some represented two or three.

The Egyptian alphabet had no signs for vowels. This presents a problem for readers of hieroglyphs. No one has ever heard ancient Egyptian spoken out loud, so no one has any idea where the vowels go or even which vowels to use. This is like seeing the

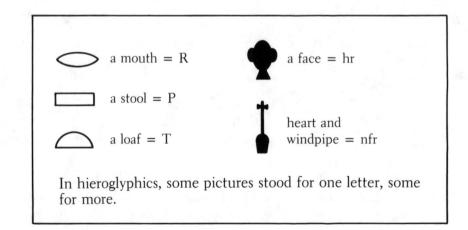

In hieroglyphics, some pictures stood for one letter, some for more.

letter *t* for the English word "at" and wondering if the word is at, et, it, ot, ut, ta, te, ti, to, or tu. And that's not even counting double-vowel combinations like ate, tea, ita, and so forth.

This may be why the ancient Egyptians often added determinatives—extra hieroglyphs to make the meaning of a word clearer. For example, the letters h, n, and w could mean a liquid measure, rejoicing, or neighbors. So the scribe added a picture of a beer pot when writing "liquid measure," a happy man when writing "rejoicing," and a man and a woman when writing "neighbors."

The earliest Egyptian writing that has come down to us is over five thousand years old. It is a combination of picture words, sounds, and determinatives. It can be read from right to left, left to right, or top to bottom. The people and animals in the hieroglyphs are always facing the beginning of a line. There is no punctuation,

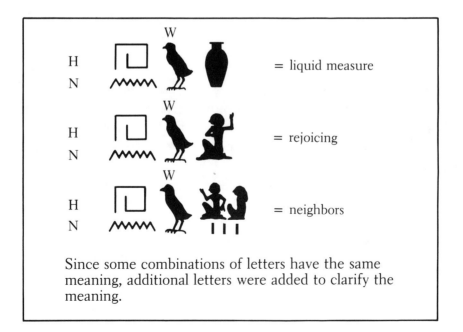

Since some combinations of letters have the same meaning, additional letters were added to clarify the meaning.

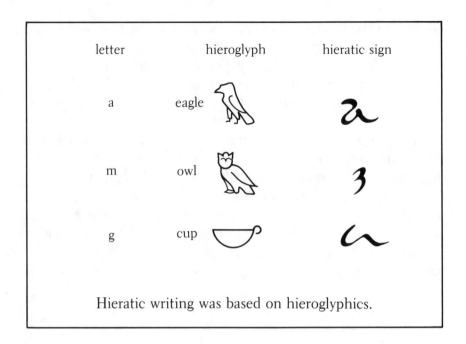

letter	hieroglyph	hieratic sign
a	eagle	
m	owl	
g	cup	

Hieratic writing was based on hieroglyphics.

although the beginning of a new sentence or word may be in a different color.

Around 2500 B.C. a faster Egyptian "shorthand" was invented. This writing, called **hieratic script**, was based on hieroglyphs, but fewer strokes were used. Hieratic became the everyday script; the more elegant hieroglyphs were kept for inscriptions on monuments or other formal occasions.

The Egyptians invented one of the earliest writing systems in history. They also discovered the best portable writing material in the ancient world—**papyrus**. Papyrus is a reed which was once plentiful along the banks of the Nile River. No one knows who the unknown genius was who first split the stem of the reed and sliced it into thin strips. The strips were laid side by side and then another layer of strips was placed on top at right angles to the original layer. When the papyrus was beaten, the layers stuck together forming a crude sheet of paper. The sheet was dried and then polished by rubbing it with stone or ivory. Glued together, papyrus sheets formed long scrolls which were wrapped around one or two sticks. These scrolls, called *volumen*, were the world's first books. The English words "paper" and "volume" come from these Egyptian inventions.

Papyrus also supplied the first pens for Egyptian scribes; a thin reed with a crushed end dipped in ink was used to brush letters onto a page. Later, a stylus, or pen with a sharp point, was invented.

Black ink was first used in Egypt about 2000 B.C. It was made from the soot of oil lamps mixed with vegetable gum. Red ink also had a gum base, but the color came from the red mineral ochre. The Egyptians also had a special ink for writing on linen—an early ancestor of the modern laundry marking pen!

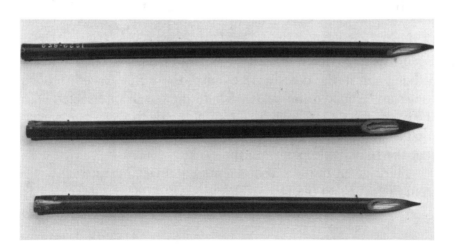

Reed pens used for writing script. (The number on the top pen is the museum's catalog number.)

AGRICULTURE

Ancient Egyptians believed that after death a judge would ask them three questions before admitting them to eternal life. They would have to swear that they had not murdered, robbed, or built a dam during their time on earth. This does not mean that the Egyptians were opposed to irrigation. On the contrary, they did everything they could to take advantage of Egypt's limited water supply. That's why no individual was allowed to build a dam; the government strictly regulated every drop of water.

The very first Egyptian farmers waited for the natural overflow of the Nile to water the crops. However, as early as 5000 B.C. they had begun to figure out ways to control the great river. In doing this, they invented the world's first irrigation system. They began by digging canals to direct the Nile flood to distant fields. (One of the first official positions in the Egyptian government was that of "canal digger.") Later, they constructed reservoirs to contain and save the water for use during the dry season. The first reservoir in Egypt—and the first in the world—was at Fayum, a low-lying area of the desert. During flood season Fayum became a lake. The Egyptians built about 20 miles (30 km) of dikes around Fayum. When gates in the dikes were opened, the water flowed through canals and irrigated the fields. Where the canals intersected with the river, dams were built. The tops of the dams were leveled and used as roads. During the flood season the dams were broken so that the river could pour into the canals.

The ancient farmers also invented a device for moving water from the canals to the fields. This was a **shaduf**—a long pole bal-

Drilling for water in modern Egypt—the traditional way

anced on a horizontal wooden beam. At one end of the pole was a weight and at the other was a bucket. The weight made it easier to raise a quantity of water for irrigation or drinking.

Some historians believe that the Egyptians were also the first people to use a plow. Early tomb paintings show a bow-shaped stick that was dragged along the ground. Later, human beings were harnessed to the plow. One wall painting shows four people pulling and one directing the tool. By 2000 B.C. oxen had taken over the heavy work. The harness was first slipped over the animals' horns; eventually a neck collar was invented that did not interfere with the animals' breathing.

After workers sowed the seed, goats or oxen were sent into the fields to trample it into the dirt. When the grain was ripe, the farmers harvested it with sickles. The sickles were made of wood and had pieces of flint glued to the cutting edge. Workers then threw the grain into the air over and over again with wooden scoops. The heavy grain fell to the ground while the wind blew the lighter seed covering away.

The Egyptians also grew a variety of fruit and vegetables, including onions, dates, olives, figs, and grapes. They brewed beer by mixing crumbled barley cakes with yeast, honey, and water and allowing the mixture to stand for a few days. They also made wine from grapes, dates, or palm sap. The grapes and dates were trampled by barefoot workers, and the palm trees were tapped near the base. The juice was sealed inside pottery jars until it fermented.

The Egyptians were also among the first ancient peoples to domesticate animals. That is, they tamed several wild species and then bred them in order to supply food and labor. Long-horned African cattle, sheep, oxen, goats, pigs, and donkeys were first

Working the soil

68

domesticated in Egypt. The Egyptians also kept antelopes, geese, ducks, and bees, which were valued for their honey and wax.

The Egyptians knew how to preserve meat by drying it in the sun or in the salt compound natron. They were also the first people to make leather. Archaeologists have found bodies wrapped in tanned leather garments dating from 3800 B.C. The leather was made by scraping animal hides with a special tool and treating them with a solution of alum and salt.

CRAFTS AND TECHNOLOGY

The tombs of many Egyptian rulers contained little ceramic or pottery figures called ushebtis. Each ushebti represented a worker who was to serve the pharaoh for all eternity. Since the next life was believed to be similar to this one, all kinds of workers were provided. There were tiny weavers, potters, goldsmiths, sailors, and many others. The ushebtis were placed in model rooms with their tools and supplies, leaving future generations a perfect record of Egyptian crafts and technology.

POTTERY AND BRICKS

Pottery was produced in Egypt from the earliest times. Potters mixed the clay by walking on it; they formed vases and bowls by coiling strings of clay into various shapes. Clay was also pressed into molds or simply pinched into shape. Later, the Egyptians began to use a type of potter's wheel that could be turned by hand.

At first clay was baked in an open fire, but by 3000 B.C. Egyptian potters were using kilns made of clay and rock. These were tall structures with a clay floor pierced by a number of vents.

Under the floor the potters built a fire. The heat rose through the body of the kiln, where the pottery was stacked, and the smoke escaped from a hole in the top. Some kilns were made with an outer platform on one wall; the potters stood on this to fill and unload the kiln.

Kilns were sometimes used to fire bricks, but the desert sun is so strong that this was not really necessary. Bricks were the basic building material of the common people. Everyone mixed sand, straw, and mud and left it outside to dry when they were constructing a house. The earliest bricks were shaped by hand; later a rectangular wooden mold was used. The Egyptian word for brick, *tobe*, has passed into our language as adobe.

GLASS

After a long, weary day, a Phoenician merchant traveling in the Egyptian desert stopped to make camp. When he had finished cooking, he put the hot pot containing his dinner on top of a pile of natron. A few minutes later he picked up the pot and found glass!

That's the story Pliny, an ancient Roman writer, told about the discovery of glass. Although melted natron does form a glasslike substance, Pliny was probably wrong. Glass was first used in Mesopotamia; it was not manufactured in Egypt until around 1500 B.C. Egyptian glass was used for small containers and for jewelry. It was even made into imitation precious stones. The glass was clear or colored with minerals such as copper, cobalt, and iron.

*Drawings of 3,500-
year-old glass vases*

Egyptian glassmakers did not know how to blow glass. However, they had several other methods of shaping their material. Sometimes they filled a cloth bag with sand and dipped it into a vat of molten glass. Then they rolled the bag on top of a stone bench until they got the shape they wanted. When the vessel was cool, they opened the bag and poured the sand out. Sometimes the core was clay instead of sand; this was scraped out when the vessel was finished. The Egyptians also heated thin rods of glass and wrapped them around a mold. Then they reheated the glass until it fused into a single surface.

FAIENCE

Egyptian jewelry was also made from a turquoise-colored mineral called lapis lazuli. However, lapis lazuli was in short supply in Egypt. Luckily, about 4500 B.C. the Mesopotamians invented a substitute, which came to be called Egyptian **faience** because it was produced in Egypt in great quantities. Faience was made from soapstone or powdered quartz. The core mineral was covered with a glaze and fired. At first, all faience was blue, like the natural material it imitated. Later, faience was made in green, red, cream, and black varieties. It was used in jewelry, statues, tiles, and vases.

METAL AND METALWORK

Was the first human being to discover copper really searching for eye shadow? It's possible. Malachite is green, and azurite is blue. Both are ores of copper, which sometimes occurs in metallic form in deposits of these minerals. Someone may have found a lump of metal by accident, experimented with the ores, and come up with the process of making copper.

No one knows if this is really the way copper was discovered, or even who discovered it. We do know that the Egyptians were

*A jewelers' workshop. Metal is weighed,
smelted, beaten, and shaped into jewelry.*

using copper tools, weapons, and nails by 4000 B.C. In fact, copper
chisels cut the stones for the ancient pyramids. Since copper is a
relatively soft metal, each pyramid work site was surrounded by
metalworkers whose job was to melt and recast worn-out tools.

About 4,000 years ago Egyptian metalworkers learned how to
mix tin with copper to create bronze, copying a process that had

been invented by the Mesopotamians. Bronze is much more durable than copper, and it immediately became the metal of choice throughout Egypt. Tin ore does not occur naturally in Egypt, and it had to be imported.

Egypt also lacks natural iron ore, so iron was not made there until quite late in history. The Egyptians did find small amounts of iron in meteorites. Since it was so rare it was extremely precious; one of King Tut's tomb treasures was an iron dagger!

To make the metals, the earliest metalworkers placed ore in a shallow pit filled with charcoal. Assistants blew on the fire with hollow reeds in order to raise the temperature. Later, bellows made from animal skins were used for the same purpose. A worker stood with a bellows under each foot. As he stepped down on one foot, the air was forced out of that bellows. At the same time he pulled the other bellows open with a string, filling it with air and readying it for his next step.

The liquid metal was set in stone or clay molds. The "lost wax" technique was also used. A worker shaped wax into the desired form and then pressed clay around it. When the clay was fired, the liquid wax drained from a small hole in the clay. Hot metal was then poured into the same hole. After the mold cooled, the clay was broken and the metal shape was revealed.

These processes were used in many ancient cultures. However, the Egyptians really distinguished themselves in fine metalwork. Their delicate gold and silver jewelry has long been admired, and the golden statues, coffins, and face masks from ancient tombs are considered masterpieces.

STONEWORK

The world's great museums are also filled with Egyptian stonework. Besides the giant pyramids, temples and monuments, Egyp-

*Melting metal in crucibles. These workers
are operating bellows with their feet.*

tian craft workers also made delicate vases, cosmetic jars, and statues out of stone. The stone vases are particularly interesting. They are made from solid chunks of rock that were hollowed out and shaped. To do this the Egyptians probably used a drill weighted with stones with a drill bit made of flint. Coarse sand was probably sprinkled under the bit to make it cut more efficiently.

WOOD AND CARPENTRY

Another drill, weighted with stones but turned by a bow, was used by Egyptian carpenters. The ancient carpenter's workbox also included saws made of copper, flat sandstone (instead of modern sandpaper), hammers, chisels, and nails of copper or wood. Workers also used the awl (a pointed tool) and the adz (a kind of plane).

Egyptian carpenters were very skilled. They knew how to join pieces of wood in precise corners, and they could attach thin layers of attractive wood to the surface of furniture made from cheaper, plainer material. Archaeologists have even found a piece of plywood (a material made from thin layers of wood pressed together) dating from 2800 B.C.

PAINTS AND GLUES

The many minerals of the desert provided coloring for ancient Egyptian artists. Malachite was used for green. Red, yellow, and brown came from mixtures of ochre. White was produced by chalk, gypsum, or white lead. Blue was made from lapis lazuli. Since that mineral was very rare, the Egyptians developed a substitute made from silica, malachite, calcium carbonate, and natron. These colored minerals were dissolved in water and then mixed with wax or glue.

The glue was made from the skins, sinews, and bones of animals. Beeswax was another important adhesive; it was also used as a protective coating for painted surfaces.

WEAVING

Many garments sold today are advertised as "100% Egyptian cotton." They are the latest in a long line of Egyptian textile products stretching back six thousand years. Although cotton was not grown in Egypt until the Romans conquered the nation in 30 B.C., the ancient Egyptians did grow flax. The fibers of the flax plant were spun into linen, a strong, smooth thread that could be woven into delicate yet durable cloth. The Egyptians also knew how to make woolen cloth, but it was seldom used since wool was considered an unclean animal product.

Egyptian weavers spun fiber into thread on small spindles. To make cloth, one set of threads was stretched across flat looms that looked something like bed frames. The weavers used sticks to pull the cross-threads through. Later, standing looms were developed.

The bolts of fabric that have been found in tombs are of excellent quality. Most cloth was left in its original white color, although vegetable dyes were occasionally used.

BOATS

In 1969, the Norwegian explorer Thor Heyerdahl and an international crew set sail across the Atlantic Ocean in a boat made of papyrus reeds. The boat, *Ra*, had been built according to a design the Egyptians used around 3000 B.C. The Egyptians depended on the Nile for transportation, so they were pioneers of boatbuilding. The earliest known picture of a sail was found on a piece of Egyp-

tian pottery from 3200 B.C. There were several types of papyrus boats. The *Ra* was constructed of bundles of reeds lashed together with rope and powered by a linen sail. It ran into trouble, but in 1970 a similar craft, *Ra II*, made a successful trip. Heyerdahl and the other sailors were impressed by the ancient Egyptians' craft.

By around 2000 B.C., Egyptian mariners also sailed wooden boats. Cedar was often imported from Lebanon for this, since timber was scarce in the desert. The boatbuilders bored holes in the planks and laced them together with papyrus rope. Then the entire structure was covered with tar or pitch (a sticky material made from charcoal) to make it watertight. Most ships had square sails, but there was space for teams of rowers as well. A huge paddle acted as the boat's steering rudder.

Egyptian sailors carried on trade on the Mediterranean and Red seas. They also traveled up and down the Nile. Their passage into the heart of Africa, however, was limited by the cataracts on the Nile. This problem was partly solved in 2565 B.C. when canals were built around the first cataract. These canals were for navigation, not for irrigation, and it was through them that much of the stone for the pyramids was transported.

Thor Heyerdahl's papyrus boat Ra *on its attempted voyage across the Atlantic in 1969. This voyage was unsuccessful, but on the second* Ra *expedition, in 1970, Heyerdahl and his crew made it from Morocco to Barbados.*

OUR DEBT TO EGYPT

In Egypt the past is alive. The pyramids, of course, are survivors of ancient days. So is the shaduf a farmer swings out of a canal, or the mud bricks a villager sets out to bake in the sun. In some remote areas, it is still possible to find flat looms, sun clocks, and faience made according to the five-thousand-year-old process.

These are the obvious traces of the past. However, many other achievements of the early Egyptians also appear throughout the world today, in one form or another. Every time you turn a key in a lock, for example, you can thank the ancient Egyptians for keeping your valuables safe. Although the lock was not invented in Egypt, the Egyptians did design a notched key that matched pegs within the lock. This basic design is still used in today's locks. We also divide a circle into 360 degrees, as the ancient Egyptians did. In fact, the small circle used as a sign for "degree" is actually an Egyptian hieroglyph!

Possibly the most important contribution ancient Egypt has made to modern times is time itself. Our sun-based calendar comes to us from Egypt by way of Julius Caesar, who brought it to Rome in 45 B.C. So do our twenty-four-hour days, although we have abandoned changing the lengths of winter and summer hours.

The Egyptians also laid the foundations of geometry with their formulas for area and volume and their study of angles. Their practical engineering math was passed along to the Greeks when Alexander the Great conquered Egypt in 332 B.C. The Greeks extended this knowledge into theories of math—the same theories taught to schoolchildren today.

The scientific study of medicine also began in ancient Egypt. The Egyptians handed down knowledge of anatomy, drugs, and surgery to later cultures. More importantly, they passed along an attitude. Although it was mixed with magic, Egyptian medicine followed a scientific method. The ancient doctors were taught to observe, examine, diagnose, and prescribe treatment, just as doctors are taught today.

The Egyptian system of writing also has links with the present. Picture writing is still used in China and Japan, and sound symbols are the basis of our own writing system. In fact, some scholars believe that Egyptian hieroglyphs inspired the Phoenician alphabet. Phoenician letters were the ancestors of the Greek alphabet, which in turn inspired the English alphabet.

Papyrus was another important influence. Earlier writing was done only on clay or stone. These materials are not really portable—imagine carrying around a clay book! Papyrus, on the other hand, was convenient to use, store, and transport. As it became easier to comunicate in writing, government and social organization became more sophisticated. It was possible to record knowledge in books and to pass it on to others in an organized way.

As pioneers in irrigation and agriculture, the ancient Egyptians also contibuted to world culture. Consider how many "firsts" they achieved: the first to build canals and reservoirs, to use a plow, to keep cattle, sheep, oxen, goats, and donkeys.

It is not possible to prove a direct link, but it is likely that architects of later ages were inspired by the form and craftsmanship of the pyramids. The Egyptians invented many techniques for handling stone, and they were the first people to use it in monumental structures. Until the Egyptians worked with this material, no one else in the world had even laid a slab of stone on top of two columns!

Herodotus once wrote that Egypt had "wonders more than those of any other land and works . . . beyond expression great." These works have passed through more than a hundred centuries to our own time, shaping our science, our culture, and our lives.

GLOSSARY

Boning rod: A device used to level stone. A boning rod contained three poles of equal height: two fixed poles connected by string and one movable pole.

Cubit: A measure of length originally equal to the length of the pharaoh's forearm from the elbow to the tip of his middle finger.

Faience: A turquoise-colored material resembling the natural mineral lapis lazuli.

Hieratic script: A later form of Egyptian writing using fewer strokes than hieroglyphic writing.

Hieroglyph: A picture symbol used in Egyptian writing.

Natron: A salt compound used for drying meat, making mummies, and other processes.

Papyrus: A paperlike writing material made from papyrus reeds.

Pharaoh: An Egyptian king, believed to be a god.

Shaduf: A device made from a weighted pole and used for raising water.

FOR FURTHER READING

Allan, Tony. *The Time Traveler Book of Pharaohs and Pyramids.* London: Usborne, 1977.

Allen, Kenneth. *One Day in Tutankhamen's Egypt.* New York: Abelard-Schuman, 1974.

Baldwin, Gordon C. *Inventors and Inventions of the Ancient World.* Four Winds, 1973.

David, Rosalie and Anthony. *Ancient Egypt.* New York: Warwick Press, 1984.

Davies, Penelope, and Stewart, Philippa. *Tutankhamen's Egypt.* New York: St. Martin's Press, 1978.

Hoyt, Edwin P. *A Short History of Science.* New York: John Day, 1965.

Robinson, Charles A., Jr. Rev. by Lorna Greenberg. *Ancient Egypt.* New York: Franklin Watts, 1984.

Sitomer, Mindel and Harry. *How Did Numbers Begin?* New York: Crowell, 1976.

Note. The quote on page 54 was taken from *Never to Die,* by J. Mayer and T. Prideaux (New York: Viking Press, 1938), p. 51.

INDEX

ABOUT
THE AUTHOR

Geraldine Woods teaches at Horace Mann school
in Bronx, New York. She has authored and
coauthored (with her husband, Harold) over thirty
children's books, many for Franklin Watts,
including *Drug Use and Drug Abuse*, *Cocaine*, and
The Right to Bear Arms.